The
GiRLS'
Handbook

Essential Skills
A Girl Should Have

Written by Alexandra Johnson

Illustrated by Karen Donnelly

Edited by Hannah Cohen

Designed by Angie Allison

The
G RLS'
Handbook

Essential Skills
A Girl Should Have

Buster Books

The Girls' Handbook was first published in hardback
in Great Britain in 2011 by Buster Books,
an imprint of Michael O'Mara Books Limited,
9 Lion Yard, Tremadoc Road, London SW4 7NQ.
This paperback edition first published 2011.

www.mombooks.com/busterbooks

A CIP catalogue record for this book is available from the British Library.

ISBN: 978-1-907151-81-1

2 4 6 8 10 9 7 5 3 1

Papers used by Buster Books are natural, recyclable products
made from wood grown in sustainable forests. The manufacturing processes
conform to the environmental regulations of the country of origin.

Printed and bound in December 2010 by Clays Limited, St Ives plc, Popson Street,
Bungay, Suffolk, NR35 1ED, UK

CONTENTS

HOME HELP 84

EMERGENCY SKILLS 110

ARE YOU READY TO BE A SUPER-SKILLS STAR?

This book gives you the power to conquer cool skills in style and make light work of being independent for ever!

There are six sections to help you find the type of skill you want to master – from dealing with a zit in 'Everyday Essentials', to cooking spaghetti in the 'Master-chef' section or even saving someone's life using 'Emergency Skills'.

Simply follow the steps in each skill and use the pictures to help you crack the technique. You'd better get used to your new super-skill powers – your friends and family won't recognize the new you ...

SKILL SUGGESTION

As you make your way through this helpful handbook, you will come across boxes like this one. Read the information inside each one to reveal tried and tested tips and tricks that'll have you soaring to the top of the super-skills class in no time!

WARNING

These boxes contain important advice that will ensure you complete each skill safely. Always read them carefully.

EVERYDAY ESSENTIALS

SKILL 1

MAKE YOUR
TEETH SPARKLE

Follow this twice-daily routine for perfect teeth:

1. Wet the toothbrush and place a pea-sized blob of toothpaste on it.

2. Place the head of your toothbrush against your teeth, so that the bristles are at a 45° angle. Using small scooping brushstrokes, move the brush several times away from your gums, over each tooth.

3. Use the same method on the inside surfaces of your teeth.

4. To reach your back teeth, close your mouth around the brush slightly – this helps you to reach the sides of your back teeth.

5. Now brush the tops and bottoms of your back teeth using small back and forth movements.

6. Finally, brush your tongue to remove any dead bacteria – this will help keep your mouth smelling fresh all the time.

How long? How often? Brush your teeth for two minutes, twice a day.

SKILL 2

CLEAN-QUEEN HAND WASHING

A quick slosh under the tap won't get your hands germ-free. Here's how to wash them hygienically:

WHEN TO WASH?

★ After going to the loo
★ Before touching food
★ After coughing or sneezing

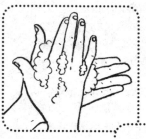

1. Wet your hands and lather up with soap by rubbing your hands together for a couple of seconds.

2. Rub your palms together in a circular motion.

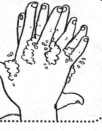

3. Rub the back of each hand with the palm of the other hand. Interlace your fingers as you do so.

4. Place your hands so that the palms are touching and interlace your fingers, as shown here. Rub your hands up and down.

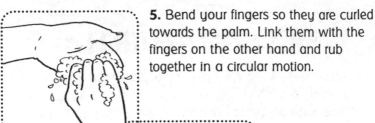

5. Bend your fingers so they are curled towards the palm. Link them with the fingers on the other hand and rub together in a circular motion.

6. Hold one thumb and rotate your hand around it.

7. Repeat with your other thumb.

8. Keeping the fingers on one hand locked together, rotate them around the whole area of the palm of the other hand.

9. Repeat with the other hand.

10. Rinse your hands in warm, running water.

11. Dry thoroughly with a towel.

SKILL SUGGESTION

Hygienic hand washing should last around 20 seconds – that's about how long it takes to sing the song 'Happy Birthday To You' twice. Practise singing the song while following the steps above. When you have finished singing the song twice, you should be on **step 10**.

TIE A TIE SMARTLY

Whether you have to wear a tie to school or just love to look stylish, learn this simple knot and you'll be able to get all dressed up without getting tied up in knots:

1. Turn up the collar of your shirt and do up the top button.

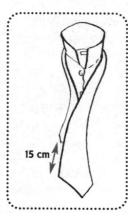

15 cm

2. Drape the tie around your neck – the wide end of the tie should be on your left if you are right-handed. (If you are left-handed. the wide end should be on your right.)

3. Pull down the wide end of the tie. so that it is roughly 15 cm longer than the skinny end.

4. Take the wide end and bring it over and under the skinny end. so that it is back on the side it started on.

The back of the wide end should now be facing out, as shown here.

5. Bring the wide end back over the top of the skinny end, as shown opposite.

6. Push the wide end of the tie up through the loop at your neck, so that the back of the wide end is facing out. You will now have made another smaller loop lower down the narrow part of the tie.

7. Push the wide end of the tie down through the new loop that you have just made in **step 6**.

8. Hold on to the skinny end and pull it down gently as you push the knot up to your collar to tighten.

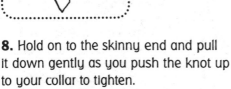

SKILL 4

STEPS TO SHINY HAIR

Simply slopping on shampoo won't give you luscious locks. Here's how to get the shine factor:

1. Wet your hair with warm water, then massage a coin-sized amount of shampoo into your hair. (If you have very long hair, use a bit more shampoo.)

2. Flip your hair over and massage your head in circles – this helps your hair to grow well.

3. Rinse thoroughly, as any shampoo left on the hair can make it look dull.

4. Apply a coin-sized amount of conditioner to the middle and ends of your hair. Leave for five minutes.

5. Rinse thoroughly with warm water, finishing off with a quick splash of cold water.

SKILL SUGGESTION

For extra-shiny locks, warm a towel on a radiator then follow **steps 1** to **3**. Apply a thick layer of conditioner then wrap your hair in the hot towel and warm the towel with your hairdryer for ten minutes. Rinse and dry as normal.

SKILL 5

CUT AND FILE YOUR NAILS

Have smart, healthy nails for life by mastering this fabulous filing technique:

1. Soak your fingertips in warm water for two minutes.

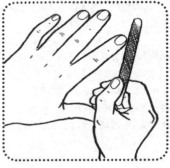

2. Cut each nail straight across the top, making sure that the nails end up roughly the same length.

3. File each nail from one side to the other to smooth them into a rounded shape. Try to file in one direction only.

4. Dot a small blob of petroleum jelly on to each cuticle – the skin at the base of the nail – and massage in circular movements.

5. Gently push the cuticle back towards the base of the nail using a cuticle stick – a lollipop stick works just as well.

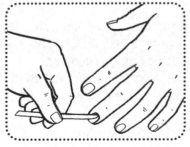

6. Remove any excess petroleum jelly from your nails by wiping them with nail polish remover.

SKILL 6

BE SAFE ONLINE

Surfing the internet from the comfort of your home can feel completely safe, but sadly there can be dangers lurking online just like in real life. Here's how to avoid them:

Keep personal details private. Don't share personal information about yourself online, even with people you view as friends.

Keep the following a secret: your full name (use a fun internet name instead), your address, your date of birth, the name of your school, your telephone number and email address.

Keep intruders out. If you have been receiving messages from people that you don't know, ask your parent or a teacher to help you block them. Don't accept friend requests from people you don't know.

Keep your computer safe. Never open emails or attachments from people that you don't know – they may contain harmful viruses that could damage your computer.

Keep your distance. Never meet someone who has contacted you online – they might not be who they say they are.

WARNING

If someone asks personal questions, or is hassling or bullying you, tell a parent, teacher or the police. Save any emails or messages from this person as proof.

SKILL 7

MANAGE YOUR MONEY

Don't pour your pennies down the drain – follow these tips and watch the pennies grow into pounds, pounds, pounds!

Think twice. Do you really want that new skirt? Think about it for a whole week before you buy it – this way you'll know if it's just a passing whim or a sensible decision. If you really want it, start saving up and buy it when you know you can afford it.

Open a bank account. Ask your parents to help you to set up a young person's bank account. This way your pennies are harder to get hold of and you'll have time to decide if you really need something.

Earn it. Ask your parents if they will pay you to do extra chores to earn yourself some extra cash. Why not offer to wash the car (see **Skill 30**) or clean the windows (see **Skill 70**) for some extra pocket money of course?

SKILL 8

LACE UP AND TIE YOUR SHOES

This is an easy way to lace shoes that will make sure they look smart and neat:

LACE THEM UP RIGHT

1. Put one of your shoes on the correct foot. (You may find it easier to lace up your shoes while your foot isn't inside them – if so, place a shoe on the floor in front of you with the toe facing away from you.)

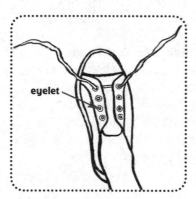

2. Thread the shoelace down through one of the eyelets closest to the toe.

3. Pull the shoelace across and up through the opposite eyelet.

4. Pull the ends of the shoelace until they are the same length.

5. Working in a diagonal direction, insert the right end of the shoelace into the next hole on the left from underneath and pull it through.

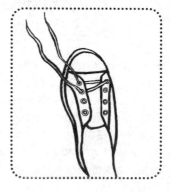

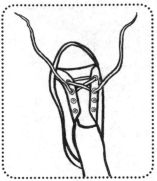

6. Insert the left end of the shoelace into the next hole on the right.

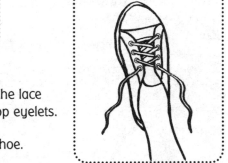

7. Continue criss-crossing the lace ends until you reach the top eyelets.

8. Repeat with the other shoe.

TIE THEM UP TIGHT

Follow the steps below to tie the laces in a bow. (Put your shoes on now if you put the laces in without your feet inside the shoes.)

1. Hold both ends of the shoelaces – one in each hand – and cross them over.

2. Place a finger under the point where the shoelaces cross over each other.

Tuck one end of the shoelace under and pull it towards you to make a knot, as shown here.

3. Place an index finger on the knot.

4. Make a large loop with one of the shoelace ends and hold it at the base with two fingers.

5. Wrap the other lace around the loop you just made in **step 4**.

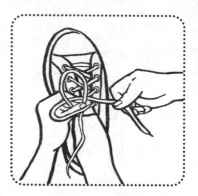

6. Use a finger to poke the middle of the lace back through the loop, pulling it towards you to make a second large loop.

7. Pull both loops to tighten the bow you have just made and secure your shoelaces, so they stay tied all day long!

SKILL 9

AVOID TRAVEL SICKNESS

Follow these tips for a trouble-free tummy:

BEST PLACE TO SIT IF YOU ARE ...

... in a car. Sit in the front passenger seat.

... on a boat. Sit up on deck or in the middle of the boat.

... on a plane. Sit in a window seat over a wing.

DO get fresh air by opening a window, if you can.

DON'T look out of the window at other moving cars if you are travelling in a car. Instead, try to focus on a fixed point on the horizon.

DON'T read or play games.

DO eat or drink ginger or peppermint flavoured food or drink.

DO drink plenty of water to keep you hydrated throughout the journey.

SKILL 10

GET PERFECTLY POLISHED SHOES

If your shoes shine, you'll shine too. Here's the best way to polish them to perfection:

1. Place your shoes on some old newspaper on the floor. (If your shoes have laces, take them out.) Wipe the shoes with a damp cloth to remove any dirt and leave them to dry.

2. Wrap a soft, dry cloth around your index and middle finger. Dip it in some shoe polish – use shoe polish that is the same colour as your shoes, or use a clear shoe polish. (Never use polish on suede shoes. Clean them with a stiff brush instead.)

3. Rub the cloth on one shoe in small circular motions, starting from the heel, until the whole shoe is covered in a thin layer of polish. Do the same to the other shoe.

4. Leave the shoes to dry for as long as possible to allow the polish to absorb.

5. Put one hand inside one shoe and, with the other hand, briskly brush all over with a shoe brush. This process is called 'buffing' and will make your shoes really shine. Do the same to the other shoe.

6. Repeat **steps 2** to **5**. (Put the laces back in if your shoes have them.)

SKILL 11

MAKE YOUR TRAINERS SMELL SWEET

Stinky trainers can be a blush-making problem, but with these rules you can bust that odour for good:

STOP SMELLS IN THEIR TRACKS

Rule 1. Make sure your feet are clean by washing them every day. Remember to dry them thoroughly, especially between your toes.

Rule 2. If your trainers get wet, leave them somewhere airy, such as a garage, and don't wear them again until they are fully dry.

Rule 3. Wear thick socks made from natural fibres, such as cotton, as these will absorb moisture better than synthetic fabrics.

HOME-MADE ODOUR-EATERS

If the smell won't shift, make your own odour-eaters. Here's how:

1. Find an old pair of socks and fill each one with a few tablespoons of bicarbonate of soda.

2. Secure each sock at the ankle by tying a ribbon around it and securing it in a bow. Cut off the rest of the fabric on each sock.

3. Place an odour-eater in each trainer overnight. By morning they should be pong-free!

SKILL 12

STAY SAFE IN THE SUN

The sun's rays contain harmful UV (ultraviolet) light that can damage your skin. Follow this advice and enjoy the sun the smart way:

DO apply sunscreen about 15 to 20 minutes before you leave the house. Wear a sunscreen with a sun protection factor (SPF) of at least 30, and reapply at least every two hours to every part of your body that is in the sun. Reapply whenever you've been swimming.

DON'T stay in the sun between 11 a.m. and 3 p.m. on a hot day.

DO drink plenty of water while you are in the sun and after you come inside. Sunshine can leave you feeling tired and dehydrated.

DO wear a hat to shade your face and sunglasses with a good UV rating to protect your eyes.

DON'T be fooled by cloud cover – harmful rays can still get through and burn your skin even on a cloudy day.

SKILL 13

EAT RIGHT EVERY DAY

Eating healthily doesn't just help your body develop properly, but helps you to zing with energy, too! Use the guide below to help you eat right every day of the year:

Eat five portions a day of ... fresh fruit and vegetables.

Fill up on ... jacket potatoes, pasta, bread and cereal.

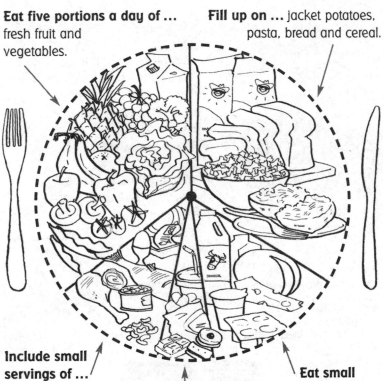

Include small servings of ... baked beans, roast chicken, eggs, meat, fish and nuts.

Enjoy these treats only occasionally ... chocolate, fizzy drinks, crisps, cakes and biscuits.

Eat small portions every day of ... cheese, yogurt and milk.

SKILL 14

DEAL WITH A ZIT

Deal with dreaded zits and stop them in their tracks:

1. Put a mirror in a well-lit area, such as on a windowsill.

2. Wash your hands thoroughly (see **Skill 2**).

3. If the spot has no white or black 'head', go straight to **step 5**.

4. Wrap each of your index fingers inside a clean tissue, and use these fingers to gently push into the middle of the spot from either side – this should squeeze out any 'pus' (white or yellow gunk) inside.

If nothing comes out, stop squeezing – you don't want to irritate your skin.

5. Mix two drops of tea tree oil with 150 ml of warm water. Soak a cotton wool ball in the mixture then dab it on the spot.

6. Leave the area to dry completely.

SKILL SUGGESTION

Stop Ziwot rearing their ugly heads by eating healthily. Turn to **Skill 13** to learn how to eat a healthy diet and make sure your skin stays glowing.

SKILL 15

GET RID OF HICCUPS

Hic … hic … hiccups aren't just noisy and annoying – a bad case could leave you seriously red in the face. Read on to find out how to shut them up:

WHAT ARE 'HICCUPS'?

★ Hiccups happen when muscles spasm in your throat and chest.

Try the remedies below until your hiccups stop:

• Hold your breath and swallow fast three times. This is more difficult than it sounds, but it might do the trick.

• Bite on a lemon or swallow a spoonful of granulated sugar.

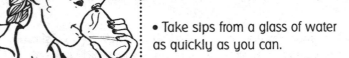

• Take sips from a glass of water as quickly as you can.

SKILL 16

SNEEZE WITHOUT SPREADING DISEASE

Sneezes and coughs can really spread germs around, so make sure you bust those germs before they cause more trouble! Here's how:

1. When you feel a sneeze coming, turn your face away from anyone who is near you.

2. Sneeze into a clean tissue – not your hands.

3. If your hands do get covered by the snot, wash them thoroughly straight afterwards (see **Skill 2**).

4. Fold the tissue over once then throw it straight into the bin. Use a fresh tissue every time you sneeze.

SKILL SUGGESTION

If you're suffering from a cold, take a bunch of tissues with you at all times to avoid a snotty situation.

WARNING

You may love your best friend so much that you'd share anything with her ... but never share used hankies!

SKILL 17

PACK YOUR BAG FOR SUCCESS

Do mornings find you racing around, trying to eat toast while drying your P.E. kit with a hairdryer? Yes? Then transform your life with these packing tips:

• Always pack your bag the night before school or a day trip.

• Take everything out of your bag and throw away any rubbish. Remove items you don't need for the next day.

SKILL SUGGESTION

Put soft food items such as bananas in a hard box to avoid the bottom of your bag getting covered in mush and goo.

• Check your homework book to see if you have any reminders to take special equipment, such as cookery items or your P.E. kit.

• If you have plans to go anywhere after school, remember to pack a change of clothes if you need to.

• Before you leave in the morning, check out of the window to see if you'll need your umbrella or your sunglasses, or both!

• If you can't pick up your bag easily, it is too heavy. Repack it, leaving out any items you don't really need. Pack the heaviest items closest to your body – the bag will feel lighter if you do this.

MASTER-CHEF

SKILL 18

STAY SAFE IN THE KITCHEN

The kitchen is full of accidents waiting to happen, so follow these safety tips to avoid a cooking calamity:

DANGER ZONE: THE OVEN

• Always ask an adult for help when using the oven or hob.

• Don't leave the handles of hot pots and pans hanging over the cooker edge or over hot areas of the hob – they could get bumped and knocked off, or get hot and burn you.

• Wear oven gloves when touching pots and pans that are hot.

• Always keep your face back when pouring steaming-hot liquids – steam can scald.

• Stand well back when opening a hot oven door – you will be greeted by a hot blast of air.

• Turn off the oven and hob when you've finished cooking.

WARNING

If a pan catches fire while you are cooking, don't attempt to move it or put out the flames. Tell an adult, then get out of the house, stay out, and dial 999 (see **Skill 74**).

DANGER ZONE: GERMS

• When you get home from the shops, immediately put any meat, fish and dairy products in the fridge to stop them going off.

• Wash your hands before you touch any food. If you touch raw food (especially meat or eggs), always wash your hands afterwards. (See **Skill 2** to find out how to wash your hands the hygienic way.)

• Never eat cake or biscuit mixes before they are baked – they might make you ill, as it contains raw egg.

• Wash fruit and vegetables thoroughly before using them.

DANGER ZONE: CUTS

• Don't leave glasses or knives at the bottom of soapy water in the washing-up bowl – people might not see they are there and cut themselves.

• Carry knives so that the sharp end is pointing towards the floor and away from you – this way you'll be safe if you trip.

• Always pass scissors or knives to someone else handle-end first.

• Make sure chopping boards are on a stable, flat surface before chopping ingredients – this will help you to control the knife when cutting, and prevent it from slipping.

SKILL 19

PEEL AN ORANGE

Here's the non-fiddly, quick way to peel a lovely juicy orange:

1. Roll the orange around on a chopping board – this will loosen up the skin and make it easier to peel.

WARNING

Always ask an adult to help you when using sharp knives.

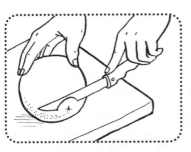

2. Hold the orange on its side and, with a sharp knife, carefully slice off the top. (The top of the orange has a little brown dent where the stalk used to be.)

3. Slice off the bottom end of the orange in the same way.

4. Cut the orange in half and then cut each part in half again.

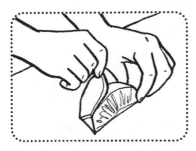

5. Peel the skin off each quarter and enjoy each orangey piece.

SKILL 20

BOIL AN EGG

Follow these simple rules for a perfect boiled egg every time:

WARNING

Always ask an adult to help when using the hob, and take extra care when using boiling water.

TO MAKE SOFT-BOILED EGGS

1. Take your egg out of the fridge about an hour before you want to cook it – this is because very cold eggs may crack when they touch hot water.

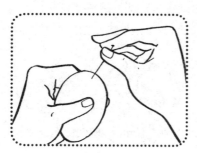

2. Make a tiny pin prick in the shell at the fattest end of the egg – this will let steam escape while it cooks.

3. Pour water into a saucepan – enough to cover the whole egg by roughly 1 cm.

4. Heat the water so that it is gently simmering – this means just bubbling.

5. Slowly lower the egg into the water with a tablespoon.

6. Turn on a timer and cook the egg for four minutes – this will give you a soft, runny yolk.

If you like a firmer yolk, set the timer for six minutes instead.

7. Turn the hob off, then remove the egg from the pan with the tablespoon and place it in an egg cup.

8. Slice away the top of the egg shell using the edge of a teaspoon to reveal the yummy yolk inside. Why not serve with hot, buttered toast cut into slices?

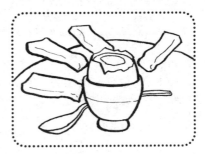

TO MAKE HARD-BOILED EGGS

1. Repeat **steps 1** to **5** on the opposite page.

2. Put on the timer and cook the egg for seven minutes, then turn the hob off.

3. Remove the egg with a teaspoon and hold it under cold, running water to cool it down, then leave in a bowl of cold water for two minutes.

4. Peel away the shell of the egg. Cut the egg into quarters, and serve with a fresh, crispy salad for an 'egg-straordinarily' tasty lunch!

SKILL 21

CHOP AN ONION

Chop an onion chef-style by following this crafty technique:

WARNING

Always ask an adult to help you when using sharp knives.

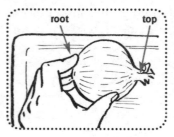

1. Place the onion on its side, on a chopping board.

If you are right-handed, the root should be on the left-hand side and the top on the right, as shown here.

If you are left-handed, turn the onion so that the root end is on your right.

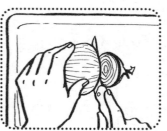

2. Using a sharp knife, slice off the top of the onion.

3. Peel off the crispy outer layer of brown skin and throw it away or put it in the compost bin.

4. Cut the onion in half down its middle, from the top to the root.

5. Place one onion half, with the cut side face down, on the chopping board.

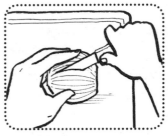

6. With the knife pointing towards the root, hold the onion with your other hand and carefully slice downwards, starting from the root end and finishing at the top end to make a series of horizontal cuts. Repeat until all the onion is sliced.

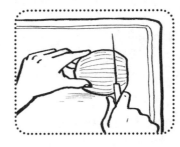

7. Using your fingers to hold the sliced sections together, turn the knife and slice all the way across the onion, to make a series of vertical cuts.

Repeat until you reach the root. Throw away the root or put it in the compost bin.

8. Repeat **steps 5** to **7** with the other onion half.

SKILL SUGGESTION

Do you find yourself fighting back the tears when chopping up onions? This is because vapours that make your eyes water are released from the onion when you cut into it.

To reduce the tears, peel the skin off the onion then soak it in water for half an hour before you chop it. Avoid rubbing your eyes when you are handling it.

SKILL 22

PEEL A POTATO

Learn how to peel a potato perfectly by following the steps below:

WARNING

Be very careful when using a sharp vegetable peeler.

1. Hold the potato in your left hand if you are right-handed, or in your right hand if you are left-handed.

2. Hold the peeler firmly in your other hand.

Position the blade so that it is on the top of the potato.

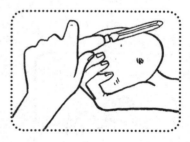

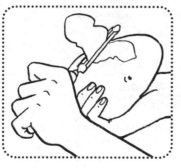

3. Push the peeler downwards and stroke it away from you. Peel the rest of the top half of the potato in this way.

4. Turn the potato around and peel the other half in the same way.

5. Turn the potato over and repeat **steps 3** and **4** on the ends.

6. Rinse the potato under the cold tap, then put your potato peelings in the waste or compost bin.

SKILL 23

MAKE A SMOOTHIE

If you're having a friend over to your house, why not impress her by whipping up a delicious smoothie? Here's how:

WARNING

Always ask an adult to help you when using a blender.

YOU WILL NEED

- 1 ripe banana, cut in half
- 1 small glass of milk
- 1 small pot of natural yogurt
- 1 small glass of frozen berries
- 1 tsp of honey

Serves 2 people.

1. Put all the ingredients together in a blender.

2. Make sure the lid of the blender is firmly in place, then switch the blender on.

3. Blend until the mixture is smooth and there are no big lumps of fruit.

4. Split between two glasses and serve.

SKILL SUGGESTION

Why not make your own signature smoothie by experimenting with lots of different ingredients? Try using ice cream instead of yogurt for a deliciously creamy smoothie.

> SKILL 24

COOK SPLENDID SPAGHETTI

Learn to cook spaghetti and you'll never need to put up with a rumbling tummy again:

WARNING

Always ask an adult to help you when using the hob.

---

1. Fill a large saucepan with water and place it on the hob. Switch on the heat and bring the water up to the boil – so that you can see the water bubbling.

2. Measure out roughly 75 g of spaghetti per person for adults and roughly 50 g for children.

3. Hold all of the spaghetti at one end. Put the other end into the pan until the spaghetti touches the bottom.

Be careful not to get splashed by the hot water when you put the spaghetti into the pan. Keep your hand well away from the water.

4. After a few moments, use a wooden spoon to push the spaghetti further into the water as it starts to soften.

5. Check the cooking instructions on the spaghetti packet and set a timer accordingly – it is usually nine to ten minutes.

6. When the timer goes off, use a fork to take out a piece of spaghetti from the pan. Blow on it, then taste it to test if it is ready. Be careful – it will be very hot so wait for it to cool down.

Perfectly cooked spaghetti should be soft but still firm – this is called 'al dente'. That means it's soft enough to eat, but is still firm when you bite into it. If you like your spaghetti softer, just cook it for a minute or two more Turn off the hob when it is cooked.

7. Place a colander in the sink and, using oven gloves, take the pan off the hob and pour the contents into it. The boiling water will drain away.

8. Shake the colander from side to side until the spaghetti has drained thoroughly. It is now ready to eat.

SKILL SUGGESTION

To serve, heat up a jar of pasta sauce by following the instructions on the label, then mix it into the spaghetti. Grate some cheese on top for some added flavour. Now tuck in!

SKILL 25

MAKE AND TOSS PANCAKES

Pancakes are a great snack, not just on Pancake Day, but any day of the week. Read on to find out how to make them:

WARNING

Always ask an adult to help you when using the hob.

YOU WILL NEED

- 110 g plain flour
- a pinch of salt
- 2 eggs • 200 ml milk mixed with 75 ml of water
- 50 g unsalted butter

Makes 12 to 14 pancakes.

1. Sift the flour and salt into a large bowl.

2. Make a small hollow in the flour and crack the eggs into it. (See **Skill 26** to find out how to crack an egg.)

3. Mix the egg and flour using a whisk. Gradually pour the milk mix into the bowl, whisking all the time – you should now have a smooth batter with no lumps of flour.

4. Choose a light frying pan for flipping – a heavy pan will be a strain on your wrist.

5. Melt the butter in the frying pan on the hob.

6. Once all the butter has melted, pour it into the batter and mix thoroughly. Turn the heat up under the pan.

7. Use a big spoon or a ladle to pour a small amount of batter into the centre of the pan.

8. Tilt the pan around so that the batter covers the whole of the bottom of the pan in a thin layer.

9. Let it cook for about one minute, then shake the pan from side to side to make sure that your pancake slides around freely.

10. With the handle firmly gripped in both hands, hold the pan out in front of you and move away from the hob.

With a quick, smooth movement flick the pan up and down so that the pancake flips up and over and lands back in the pan – this takes practice to perfect.

11. Let the pancake cook for one minute, then slide it from the pan on to a plate.

12. Repeat **steps 7** to **11** to make more pancakes. If the pancakes start to stick to the pan, add a small knob of butter to the pan. Turn off the hob, then serve your pancakes with lemon and sugar.

SKILL SUGGESTION

If your flipping attempt fails, use a wide metal spatula to turn the pancake over.

SKILL 26

CRACKING EGGS

Breaking eggs looks tricky, but it's just a case of cracking the steps below:

1. Gently tap the egg on the side of a bowl to make a small indent in the shell.

2. Holding the egg with the fingers of both hands over the top of the bowl, push into the indent with your thumbs.

3. Once your thumbs have broken through the shell, prise the shell apart, so that the contents of the egg fall into the bowl.

SEPARATING THE WHITE FROM THE YOLK

For some recipes, you need just the yolk or just the white part of the egg. Read on, to find out how to separate the two:

1. Crack the egg, then pour the contents from one half of the shell to the other (instead of into the bowl), keeping the yolk intact but letting the white drip down into the bowl.

2. Transfer the yolk from shell to shell until all of the white part has fallen into the bowl and the yolk is left in the shell.

> **WARNING**
> Wash your hands thoroughly after touching raw egg (see **Skill 2**).

SKILL 27

BREW A PERFECT POT OF TEA

Making a pot of tea using tea bags or tea leaves is a fine art. Here's how to make the perfect brew:

1. Empty your kettle and fill it with fresh, cold water, then boil.

WARNING

Always ask an adult to help you when using boiling water.

2. Pour a small amount of the freshly boiled water into a teapot. Gently swoosh the pot around in a circular motion so that the hot water warms it up, then pour the water away.

3. Put one tea bag or one teaspoon of tea leaves per person into the pot. Add one extra tea bag or teaspoon of leaves, then fill the pot with the remaining water from the kettle. Stir the pot then put the lid back on.

4. Leave to brew for no more than three minutes – longer than this will make the tea taste bitter.

5. Holding the lid firmly in place with one hand, pour the tea into cups – use a strainer to catch the tea leaves if you have used them. Serve with chilled milk and sugar if liked.

SKILL 28

SET THE TABLE

If you are asked to set the table for dinner, here's how to do it the restaurant way:

a. Place a fork to the left of the main course plate. If you are having a starter, place a smaller fork, called a 'starter fork', to the left of it.

b. Place a knife to the right of the plate. If you are having a starter, place a smaller knife, called a 'starter knife', to the right of it. If you are having soup as a starter, place the soup spoon here (**c**).

d. Place a dessert spoon along the top of the plate, with the handle on the right. Place a dessert fork below it, with the handle on the left.

e. Place glasses above the knives and to the right.

f. Place a side plate to the left of the forks for bread. Fold a napkin in half and place a butter knife on top.

SKILL 29

MAKE A SPONGE CAKE

**Once you've perfected this recipe, this basic cake
is a truly tasty tea-time treat:**

YOU WILL NEED

• 175 g self-raising flour • 1 tsp baking
powder • 3 large eggs • 175 g caster sugar
• 175 g butter, plus extra for greasing
• ½ tsp vanilla extract • jam of your choice
• icing sugar for dusting

WARNING

Always ask an adult to help you when using the oven.

1. Take your butter out of the fridge at least two hours before you start cooking, so that it warms up to room temperature.

2. Pre-heat the oven to 170°C / 325°F / Gas Mark 3.

3. With a small amount of butter, grease two sponge tins that are 20 cm in diameter.

4. Line each sponge tin with a circle of greaseproof paper.

To do this, put the tin on top of the paper and cut around the bottom of the tin to get it the right size.

5. Sift the flour and baking powder into the mixing bowl.

This sifting process adds air to the flour, which will make your cake light and fluffy.

6. Crack the eggs into the flour. (Turn to **Skill 26** to find out how to crack an egg.)

7. Add the sugar, the butter and the vanilla extract.

8. Use a wooden spoon to mix everything together until it's smooth.

9. Split the mixture evenly between your two sponge tins. Smooth the surfaces down with the flat edge of a knife.

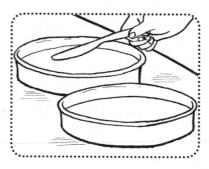

10. Place both sponge tins carefully on to the middle shelf of the oven and bake for 30 minutes – do not open the oven door during this time as this could prevent the cakes from rising.

11. After 30 minutes, use oven gloves to remove the tins and place them both on a wire cooling rack.

12. Check to make sure that each cake is cooked. To do this, insert a knife into the centre of each cake. If the knife comes out clean with no bits of cake mixture sticking to it, the cake is cooked. Turn off the oven and go straight to **step 13**.

> **WARNING**
>
> Be very careful not to touch the cake tins – they will be hot.

If your cakes need longer to cook, carefully place them back in the oven for another five minutes and then repeat the test above. Turn off the oven when your cakes are ready.

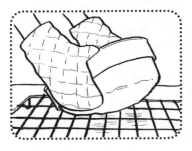

13. After five minutes, put on your oven gloves and carefully turn out the cakes upside-down on to the wire cooling rack. Peel off the paper and leave to cool completely.

14. Once cool, turn one cake over and spread a thick layer of jam on top. Carefully place the other sponge on top of it.

15. Using a sieve, dust the top of your super sponge cake with icing sugar and serve.

DO-IT-YOURSELF

SKILL 30

WASH A CAR

Become a top-class car washer and you could soon double your pocket money by offering your cleaning services to your family and neighbours:

YOU WILL NEED

- a pair of rubber gloves
- a hose connected to a tap (if available) • 2 buckets
- car shampoo • a sponge
- a stiff brush • a chamois leather (or a clean, smooth cloth will do) • 2 clean, smooth cloths
- car wax • a vacuum cleaner

1. Pop on some old clothes and a pair of rubber gloves.

2. Attach a garden hose to the nearest outdoor tap, and hose down the whole of the car – this should remove most of the dust and mud. (If you don't have a hose, use a bucket of water and a cloth.)

3. Fill one bucket with clean, cold water from the tap and the other one with a mixture of car shampoo and warm water.

4. Soak your sponge in the soapy water and clean the roof of the car by moving your sponge in big, circular movements.

5. Sponge down the rest of the car in the same way in the following order: windows, doors, bonnet, boot, hubcaps and wheels. When the sponge gets dirty, dip it in the bucket of cold water to rinse it. When the bucket of cold water looks dirty, change the water.

6. Use the brush to scrub the mud out of the tyres and hubcaps. Do not use it on the paintwork, as it may cause damage.

7. Rinse off all the bubbles on the car using the hose or a bucket of clean, cold water. Dry the windows and paintwork off by wiping all over using the chamois leather.

8. Dip a smooth cloth in the car wax and rub it gently into the paintwork, doing a small area at a time. The wax will make the paintwork look 'cloudy'. Use the other smooth cloth to rub the wax until the car looks really shiny. This is called 'buffing'.

9. Finish off your super car-cleaning service by vacuuming the seats and floor inside the car.

Step back and admire your handiwork.

WARNING

Always ask an adult to help you when using electrical equipment, such as vacuum cleaners.

SKILL 31

THREAD A NEEDLE

Before you can fix any clothes, you need to master the skill of threading a needle:

1. Hold the needle against a white piece of paper so that you can see where the hole or 'eye' is.

2. Cut a length of thread (roughly the length of your arm) and gently lick one end to wet it – this stops the fibres from fraying and makes it easier to thread through the eye of the needle.

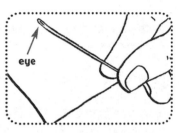

3. Holding the needle above the paper with one hand, take the thread in your other hand and, from underneath, push it through the eye, as shown here.

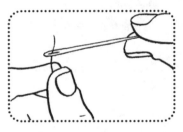

4. Hold the top of the needle near the eye in the fingers and thumb of one hand.

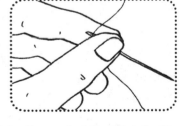

5. Take the end of the thread with your other hand and pull it through the eye, until you have a 'tail' of thread – roughly 15 cm in length. Now you are ready to sew.

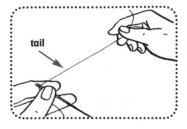

SKILL 32

PUMP YOUR BIKE TYRES

All bike tyres go flat at some point, but if you learn how to pump them up again, you'll be riding off in no time. Read on to find out how:

WHEEL KNOW-HOW

Riding your bike regularly will cause the air pressure in your tyres to go down – eventually your tyres may go flat.

Knowing the names of all the different parts on a bike wheel is a useful to skill to have, especially if you ever need to fix a puncture (see **Skill 37**). Below is a diagram of a bike wheel. Study it to familiarize yourself with the different parts, then proceed to **step 1** to find out how to pump up your tyres.

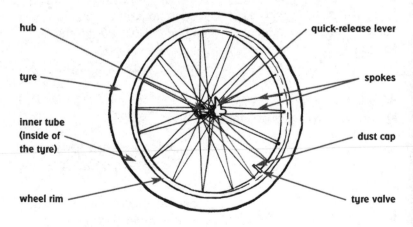

hub

quick-release lever

tyre

spokes

inner tube (inside of the tyre)

dust cap

wheel rim

tyre valve

PUMP IT UP

1. Lean your bike against a wall or balance it on its stand.

2. Use the diagram on the opposite page to help you locate where the dust cap is – the cap that covers the tyre valve.

Once you have found where it is on your bike wheel, unscrew it and keep the cap somewhere safe, such as in your back pocket.

3. Press the end of the bike pump on to the tyre valve and secure it in place.

There are many different types of bike pump – some have a clamp lever, others screw on to the valve. Refer to your pump's instruction manual for detailed instructions on how to use it if you need to.

4. Start pumping and keep going until the bike tyre is firm to the touch. Be careful not to over-inflate the tyre.

5. Remove the pump from the valve and screw the dust cap back on.

6. Repeat **steps 2** to **5** on the other tyre.

SKILL SUGGESTION

Check your tyres regularly for any damage or splits. If your tyres keep going flat you may have a 'slow puncture'. Turn to **Skill 37** to find out how to fix a puncture.

SKILL 33

CATCH A SPIDER

Spiders aren't the most popular of creatures, but there's no need to freak out if you spot one in your home. Here's the kind, fear-free way to capture a spider and release it outside:

1. Wait until the spider is on a flat surface such as a table or a wall that you can reach easily.

2. Hold a postcard in one hand and carefully place a glass over the top of the spider – be careful not to trap its legs. Hold the glass firmly in place.

3. With your other hand, slowly slip the postcard underneath the glass, lifting the glass just enough to let the card slide under it.

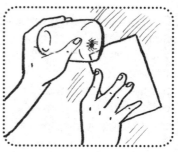

4. Keep the glass firmly clamped down on to the postcard and slide your other hand under the card.

5. Turn the glass upside down with the card held firmly on top.

6. Carry the trapped spider outside to a safe place. Put it down on the ground, postcard first with the glass on top.

7. Lift the glass away to let the spider go free.

SKILL 34

SECURE A HEM

What happens when the hem on your favourite skirt comes undone? You fix it, that's what! Here's how:

1. Check the care instructions on the skirt's label and set the iron to the recommended temperature.

2. Turn the skirt inside out and lay it on the ironing board.

WARNING

Always ask an adult to help you use an iron.

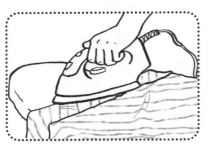

3. Following the crease, fold the hem up so that it is straight.

4. Iron the hem flat, so that it stays in the folded position.

5. Cut a 40-cm length of thread, in a colour that matches your skirt. Thread your needle (see **Skill 31**) and tie a knot in the end of the thread.

6. Push the needle up through the fabric, between the skirt and the hem, about ½ cm from the edge.

7. Pull the thread all the way through to the knot.

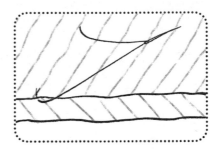

8. 'Catch' a tiny bit of the skirt's fabric with the point of your needle, about 1 cm along from its current position.

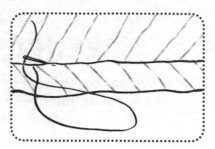

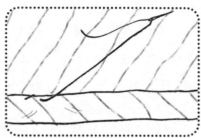

9. Push the needle back up through the edge of the hem and repeat, catching a little of the skirt's fabric 1 cm further along.

10. Repeat **steps 8** and **9** along the whole length of the hem, leaving 1 cm between stitches each time.

Don't pull the stitches too tight as this will cause the fabric to bunch up.

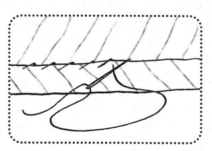

11. When you have reached the end of the skirt's hem, make several stitches in one place to secure it.

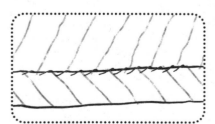

12. To be doubly certain your hem won't come undone again, tie a double knot in the end of the thread and trim the loose end. Your hem should now look like this.

SKILL 35

SEW ON A BUTTON

If a button comes loose from your favourite coat, don't panic. Follow the steps below to learn how to sew it back on:

1. Thread a needle with 50 cm of thread in a colour that matches your button (see **Skill 31** to find out how to thread a needle).

Pull the needle down to the middle of the thread and tie both ends in a double knot to secure them.

2. Position the button on top of the fabric in the place that it was originally. Check that it lines up with the buttonhole on the other side of the coat.

3. Push the needle through the fabric from underneath, into one of the holes of the button.

Pull the thread tightly.

4. Position a cocktail stick on top of the button, between the holes.

5. Pass the thread over it and push the needle through the hole opposite and then through the fabric.

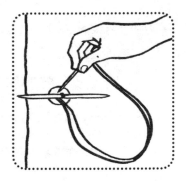

6. Pass the needle through the first hole again then back through the hole on the other side.

7. Continue sewing through each of the button's holes until you have done 15 stitches.

8. If your button is the kind with two holes, continue to **step 9**. If it has four holes, repeat **steps 6** and **7** on the other two holes,

9. Push the needle to the front of the fabric, so that your thread is now between the button and the fabric.

10. Carefully remove the cocktail stick and gently pull the button away from the coat – this will make a small space underneath. Wrap the thread around the space between the button and the fabric, at least 20 times.

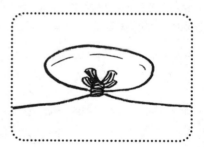

11. Push the needle through to the back of the fabric.

12. Make several stitches in one place, then cut the thread.

SKILL SUGGESTION

Why not funk up a tired coat by taking off the buttons and sewing on multi-coloured buttons instead? You could even try using buttons of different shapes.

SKILL 36

TIGHTEN A SCREW

Here's how to work some DIY magic when screws come loose and things start falling apart:

1. A screwdriver is a tool that fits into the 'head' or top of the screw. Check that you have the correct size and type of screwdriver for the job.

Screwdrivers have differently shaped heads. Opposite are the two most common shapes of screw and the type of screwdriver you will need to work with them.

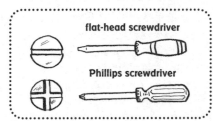

flat-head screwdriver

Phillips screwdriver

2. Hold the screwdriver in your dominant hand – the one you use for writing with. With the other hand, hold the screw in position.

3. Put the screwdriver into the grooves of the screw head and apply gentle pressure downwards, turning the screwdriver slowly.

4. To tighten a screw, turn the screwdriver to the right (clockwise). To loosen a screw, turn the screwdriver to the left (anticlockwise). To remember which way you should turn the screwdriver to tighten a screw, use this rhyme: 'Lefty loosey, righty tighty'.

5. Keep turning until the head of the screw is flat against the wood.

SKILL 37

FIX A PUNCTURE ON YOUR BIKE

If your bike's got a flat tyre and no amount of pumping is keeping it up, it might have a puncture. Follow these steps to find out how to fix one:

YOU WILL NEED

• your bike's maintenance manual • a puncture repair kit containing: rubber patches, glue, sandpaper, tyre levers (optional)
• a bucket of water
• a bike pump • chalk or a crayon • a cloth

SKILL SUGGESTION

To help you identify all of the parts mentioned in this skill, refer to the diagram of a bike wheel in **Skill 32**.

1. First, you need to check the cause of the flat tyre – it might not be a puncture, but the result of a leaky valve.

To test the valve, unscrew the dust cap on the flat tyre, and hold a cup of water under the valve, so that the valve is completely under water.

If you see bubbles in the water, this means you have a leaky valve, not a punctured tyre, and you will need to take your bike to a bike repair shop. If not, continue to **step 2**.

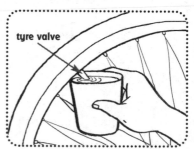

tyre valve

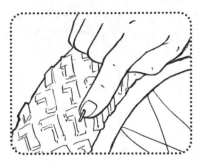

2. Inspect all around the tyre. Can you see any sharp items that may have caused the puncture? If so, carefully remove any obvious puncture causes, such as nails or thorns, wrap in a tissue and throw away, then continue to **step 3**.

3. Disengage (which means unfasten) the brakes. To do this, you will need to refer to your bike's instruction manual.

4. Next, unscrew the tyre valve (or press a button on it depending on the type of valve your bike has) to let any remaining air out of the inner tube – this is the tube that sits inside the tyre.

5. Remove the wheel by opening the quick-release mechanism that holds the wheel to the frame. To do this, pull the lever outwards, as shown on the right. (If your bike does not have a quick-release lever, refer to the bike's instruction manual to find out how to remove the wheel.)

quick-release lever

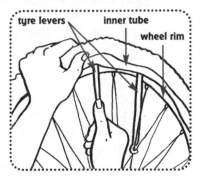

tyre levers   inner tube   wheel rim

6. Carefully pull the inner tube out from inside the wheel rim. You can use tyre levers to help prise it out if you have them.

7. Push the valve through the hole in the rim as well. (You may need to unscrew it first, depending on your bike.)

8. To find the puncture hole, listen along the length of the inner tube for a hiss of escaping air, or hold it next to your cheek and feel for a rush of air.

If you can't find the puncture hole, place sections of the inner tube into the bucket of water.

Bubbles should come out of the place where the hole is in the tube.

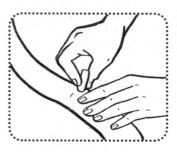

9. Mark the area of the hole with chalk, so you can find it again. Dry off the inner tube with the cloth.

10. Roughen the rubber around the puncture hole using the sandpaper from your puncture repair kit.

11. Spread a blob of glue over the hole, then leave it for a few moments until it feels 'tacky' to the touch.

12. Take the patch from your puncture repair kit and squeeze a tiny blob of glue on

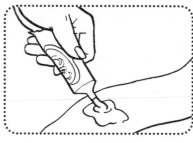

the 'contact surface' of the patch. Again, wait until it goes tacky.

13. Apply the patch over the puncture hole as if you were putting a plaster on a cut. Hold the patch on firmly for two minutes to set it in place. Smooth it down to remove any air bubbles.

14. Carefully peel away the backing sheet on the patch.

15. Dust the inner tube with chalk, especially all around the puncture patch – this stops the tube sticking to the inside of the tyre.

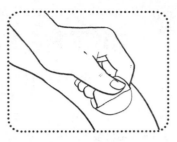

16. Pull the tyre away from the rim a little and peer inside it to look for any glass or nails. Remove any items carefully. Wrap them in a tissue and throw the tissue away.

17. Pump up the inner tube slightly – this will make it easier to fit back on the rim of the wheel.

18. Push part of the inner tube back over the wheel rim. Make sure that the valve is aligned with the hole in the wheel rim and carefully slot it back through. Make sure that it points down towards the hub.

19. Tuck the rest of the inner tube over the rim of the wheel, underneath the tyre.

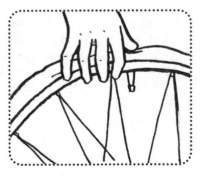

20. Use the bike pump to inflate the tyre until it is firm to touch (see **Skill 32**).

21. Fix the wheel back on to your bike by positioning it between the brake pads and closing the quick-release mechanism, if you have one.

22. Re-engage the brakes – refer to your bike's instruction manual to find out how to do this. Test that your brakes are in working order before riding off.

SKILL 38

LIFT HEAVY OBJECTS

Follow these rules and learn how to be strong and safe:

1. Look at the object to assess how easy it will be to lift. If it looks too big or too bulky in shape, or if you know the object is very heavy, don't try to lift it alone.

2. Plan the route you are going to have to carry the object along, and remove any obstructions along the way.

3. Stand in front of the object with your feet a shoulder-width apart and one leg slightly forwards – this will help you to keep your balance. Practise bending and straightening your knees, keeping your back as straight as possible.

4. When you are ready to pick the item up, slightly bend your knees – this is safer than squatting down completely or only bending your back.

5. Get a good grip on the item you want to pick up. Always hold the item underneath rather than pulling it from above.

6. Stand up in one smooth movement, letting your leg muscles pull you up and keeping your back straight. Pull your tummy muscles in too, as this strengthens your lower back.

While you're picking up or carrying the item, don't twist your back – the weight of the load could damage your spine.

7. Once you have picked up the item, see how it feels. You may need to put it down, adjust its position and try again. Hold it as close to your waist as possible and raise your arms up slightly.

8. Take small steps to get you and your item from A to B safely. Keep your head up and look forwards.

9. When you are ready to put the object down, stand with your feet a shoulder-width apart.

Use your legs to lower the object to the floor, keeping your back as straight as possible.

Do not twist your body or lean forwards as you are putting the object down.

WARNING

If you feel a twinge in your back, put the object down immediately and seek medical attention.

SMART SKILLS

SKILL 39

DE-TANGLE YOUR HAIR

**Tangled hair needn't be a pain to tame.
Here are the golden rules of de-tangling:**

1. Wet your hair with warm water, then massage a coin-sized amount of shampoo into your hair. Be careful not to pull or tug at the tangles as this will make the problem worse.

2. Rinse out the shampoo thoroughly from your hair then gently squeeze out any excess water. Massage in a coin-sized amount of conditioner. Add an extra blob directly to the really tangled areas.

3. Use a wide-toothed comb – normal combs can make tangles worse – to comb through the hair all over your head.

TOP TECHNIQUE

• Never comb from the top of your head and drag straight down, as this may pull some hairs out. Instead, hold the locks of hair in one hand and gently work the comb in between the tangles, starting near the ends and combing a little bit at a time.

SKILL SUGGESTION

Tying your hair up when playing sport or going out in windy weather will stop tangles occurring.

• You are aiming to gently untangle the hair as if it is wool that has tied in a knot, rather than just pulling the tangles out. Finally, rinse out the conditioner.

SKILL 40

APPLY PERFUME

**When it comes to scent, less is definitely more.
Use this beauty-queen method to smell just right:**

WHEN TO APPLY

★ The best time to apply perfume is after taking a shower or bath. This is because your pores will absorb the scent better.

1. Spray or dab small amounts to 'pulse points' – places where the warmth of your body will help the scent to work.

Your pulse points include: backs of the knees, inside of the elbows, on the neck, wrists and just behind the ear lobes.

2. To finish off, spray a light spritz of perfume into the air in front of you and walk through it.

SKILL SUGGESTION

Keep perfume in its original box, as harsh light or other smells can damage the scent.

SKILL 41

LOOK GOOD IN PHOTOGRAPHS

These simple tricks can make sure you look your best at the moment when someone shouts, 'Say cheese!':

Body turns. If it's a standing picture, turn your body slightly away from the camera and then turn your top half back to look at the photographer, as shown here. Put one hand on your hip instead of having both arms straight down.

Get perfect posture. Imagine that there is a tiny thread going from the bottom of your spine and out of the top of your head, pulling you gently upwards. Let your body grow taller, and relax your shoulders at the same time.

Avoid double-chin disasters. Lift up your chin and try to make sure that the camera is shooting from slightly above your face level. If the picture is taken from underneath looking up, your face will look wider than usual.

Relax and think happy thoughts. Always be yourself rather than forcing a cheesy smile for the photo. It sometimes helps to take a deep breath in through your nose and out through the mouth beforehand, to loosen up.

NO MORE NAIL-NIBBLING

Quit the habit of biting your nails in three easy steps:

1. Ask a parent to buy you some special, bitter-tasting nail polish.

2. Paint it on each nail – the taste of it will soon remind you not to nibble.

3. Once your nails have grown a bit, paint them a pretty colour – you won't want to ruin your hard work by nibbling it off again!

REMOVE A RING THAT IS STUCK

To remove a tight ring that's got stuck on your finger, follow these simple instructions:

1. Fill a bowl with cold water and tip in a whole tray of ice. Hold the hand with the ring stuck on it in the ice-water for ten seconds.

2. Dry your hand and rub plenty of hand cream in and around the ring and up the length of the finger. (If you don't have any hand cream, olive oil or washing-up liquid work just as well.)

3. Gently twist the ring and slowly work it up and over the knuckle of your finger.

SKILL 44

ANSWER THE PHONE AND TAKE A MESSAGE

Stick to the following rules whenever you answer the phone to make sure you take a message successfully:

1. When the phone rings, pick up the receiver and politely say, 'Hello'.

2. If the caller asks for someone who is not at home, ask if they would like to leave a message.

> **SKILL SUGGESTION**
>
> Keep a small notepad and pen by the side of the phone in your household.

3. If they say yes, write down the main points of the message clearly and neatly on a notepad.

4. Ask for their name and phone number. Repeat back to them the number they give to check that you have got it right, then end the call by saying, 'I will pass on your message as soon as possible. Thank you for calling.'

5. Leave the paper with the message on it somewhere that it will be seen by the person concerned, such as on the fridge.

SKILL 45

WRITE AND SEND A THANK YOU LETTER

Say 'thank you' for a special gift or occasion with a hand-penned letter. Here's how to write one and how to pop it in the post:

WRITING A LETTER

1. Using a nice pen, write your address, with one line for each part of the address, in the top right-hand corner of your paper.

2. Underneath your address, write the date.

3. On the left-hand side of the page, leaving a small space, write 'Dear [insert person's name here]'.

If it is a friend or family member, you can address them informally, for example, 'Dear Katie,'.

SKILL SUGGESTION

Keep a collection of pretty writing paper and matching envelopes in your favourite colour to use whenever you want to write to someone special.

Hill House
Honeysuckle Lane
Summerstown
Summershire
SU11 MTQ

1st August 2011

Dear Katie,

I am writing to thank you for the book tokens. I have always wanted to make my own clothes, so I will use the tokens to buy some books to help start off my new hobby.

4. Underneath this, begin your letter.

A good thank you letter conveys how thankful you are for what they have done for you, so include some details, such as, 'I am writing this letter using the beautiful fountain pen that you gave me. It is so nice to write with.'

5. Include some news to make your letter interesting to read, and finish by asking after the health of the person you are writing to.

6. Finish your letter by signing off in a way that expresses your fondness for the person, such as, 'Lots of love, [insert your name here]'.

POSTING A LETTER

1. Choose an envelope the same width as the letter that you are sending and pop your folded letter inside it.

2. Write the name of the person you are sending the letter to in the middle of the front of the envelope.

Miss Katie Johnson
1 Tree Lane
Tree-top Town
Treeshire
TU12 KTM
England

3. Below the name write the address, using a line for each part, including the country that they live in, as shown above.

4. Write your own address on the back of the envelope – if the postal service can't deliver it, they will return it to you.

5. Stick a stamp in the top right-hand corner of the envelope and pop it in a postbox.

SKILL 46

GET FRESH–SMELLING CLOTHES

Make this sweet-smelling lavender sachet and place it in your drawer to keep your clothes smelling fresh for longer:

YOU WILL NEED

• a square of pretty, patterned fabric, roughly 30 cm by 30 cm • a dessert bowl • a pencil • scissors • 80 cm length of wool • a thick, sharp needle • a handful of dried lavender (available from mail order companies)

1. Lay your fabric on a flat surface, patterned side down.

2. Place the bowl on top of the fabric in the centre of the square, face down.

3. Hold the bowl in place with one hand, then use the pencil to trace the outline with your free hand.

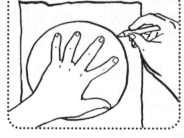

4. Remove the bowl and cut around the outline to make a circular piece of fabric.

5. Thread your needle with the wool. (See **Skill 31** to find out how to thread a needle.)

6. Turn the fabric circle over so the patterned side is facing up.

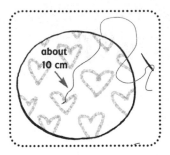

7. Make a simple stitch, by pushing the needle through the fabric at a point roughly 2 cm away from the edge of the fabric.

8. Pull the wool through the other side, leaving at least 10 cm at the end.

As you are not going to tie a knot at the end of this piece of wool until later, make sure that all the following stitches are done very loosely so that you don't pull the end through.

9. Work your way around the edge of the circle making several big, simple stitches (see **steps 7** and **8**).

Be careful not to pull the wool through too tightly.

10. Turn the fabric over.

11. Place the handful of lavender in the centre of the circle.

12. Pull on the ends of your wool to draw the fabric together to make a little pouch, as shown here.

13. Secure the wool tightly with a double knot, then tie the ends into a bow. Trim the excess wool from the ends.

14. Pop it in your drawer and you will soon have lovely, fresh-smelling clothes.

SKILL 47

ARRANGE FLOWERS

**Beautiful flowers deserve to be shown off.
Here's how to arrange them to look their best:**

1. Lay some old newspaper on a table and place the flowers on top in a row, as shown here. This will help you to see the shapes, colours and sizes of them all.

2. Choose a vase that suits the flowers. A big, multicoloured bunch will look good in a large, plain vase, a smaller bunch of thin stems may be shown off to their best in a tall, glass vase. Fill your chosen vase about a two-thirds of the way up with water.

3. Pull off any leaves near the bottom of the stalk that would be below the waterline when in the vase, then trim off 1 cm from the bottom of each stem using scissors. Cut them at a slight angle – this helps the stems to last longer.

4. Place the flowers into the vase one at a time, making sure that the stems are in the water. Crossing the stems over each other at the bottom will help them to stay in position.

5. If you have lots of different types of flower, don't bunch them together – mix them up.

6. If the water becomes cloudy after a few days, replace it. This will help the flowers to last longer.

SKILL 48

DINE IN A SMART RESTAURANT

Follow these dining 'DOs' and 'DON'Ts' to make sure you stay polite in any smart-restaurant situation:

DO sit down at your place setting, unfold the napkin and place it on your lap. Never use the napkin to blow your nose – it is to be used only for dabbing food away from around your mouth.

DON'T pull faces and make a fuss if you don't like something. Leave it on the side of your plate.

DO start using the cutlery furthest away from the plate and work your way in with each course.

DON'T reach over people to get something. Ask politely for people to pass things to you and remember to say, 'Please' and, 'Thank you'.

DO place your knife and fork neatly side by side on top of your plate at the end of each course to signal to the waiter or waitress that you have finished eating.

DON'T gobble your food. Pause to chat and take your time to enjoy the meal.

DO take a whole piece of bread from the bread basket and use the small plate next to your main plate to butter it on.

SKILL 49

WRAP A GIFT

Give all your gifts an extra-special touch with these simple steps:

1. Unroll some giftwrap, patterned side down, on to a clean table.

YOU WILL NEED

- a roll of giftwrap • scissors
- a box big enough to fit your gift inside it • sticky tape • a gift tag

2. Place the gift inside the box. Place the box upside down and in the middle of the paper.

3. Pull the edge of the giftwrap up and over the middle of the box. Then lift the paper up and over from the other side, until it overlaps by about 5 cm.

4. Cut along the paper in a straight line at this point.

5. Reposition the box in the centre of the piece of paper you have just cut.

6. Bring the longer edge of giftwrap over to the centre of the top of the box and hold it in place with your finger. Then bring the other long edge to the centre, so that the two edges overlap.

Secure it with a piece of sticky tape, as shown.

7. Turn the box over.

8. Position the box so that one of the open ends is facing you.

9. Fold the sides in as far as you can without tearing the paper.

Run your thumb along the edges of the box to make a sharp crease, so that flaps form at the top and bottom, as shown here.

10. Fold down the top flap of paper and then run your thumb down the sides to make a diagonal crease.

11. Place some sticky tape on the centre of each flap, then fold them in and secure in place.

12. Bring up the bottom flap and secure it with a piece of sticky tape. The end of the box should now be wrapped, as shown here.

13. Repeat **steps 8** to **12** with the other end of the box.

14. Write the name of the person who the gift is intended for on the gift tag in your neatest handwriting and fix it to the top of your wrapped gift. Why not fix some pretty ribbon on the top of your gift for an extra-special finishing touch?

SKILL 50

PREPARE FOR A TEST

No matter what the subject, preparing for a test can be simple if you follow these tips:

• Don't leave all your revision to the night before. Instead, slowly read through your work each day in the week before the test. Test yourself after each page to see how much you can remember.

• Write key points on some blank sticky notes – for example, how to spell 'hippopotamus' in big letters. Stick them in places where you will come across them, such as on the carton of your favourite juice – the more you look at the information, the more you will remember it!

• Get a good night's sleep the night before – your brain will be rested and ready for all the thinking it has to do (see **Skill 51**).

• Gather all the items you will need for the test and put them in your school bag the night before (see **Skill 17**). This way you will avoid getting in a fluster on the morning of your maths test if you can't find your compass!

• Eat a healthy breakfast, such as toast or cereal, as this helps to feed your brain as well as your body. Good luck!

SKILL SUGGESTION

Ask a parent or a sibling to test you. Give them your work and get them to ask you questions. If you are stuck, ask them to give you a clue before they reveal the answer.

SKILL 51

SLEEP WELL

Everyone likes to wake up feeling ready to take on the world, so here are some steps to top-quality slumber:

1. Turn off your TV or computer at least one hour before you go to bed. Using technology before lights-out time can stimulate your brain too much and keep you awake.

> ### SKILL SUGGESTION
>
> Have a cup of warm milk or camomile tea half an hour before bedtime. These drinks calm and soothe your body, ready for sleep.

2. Use your bed for sleeping in only – do not do any last-minute homework under the duvet or talk to your friends on the phone. This way your brain will think 'sleep' as soon as you get into bed.

3. Get your room the right temperature – if it's too hot you will toss and turn during the night. Slightly cool is best, because it will make you feel nice and snuggly under the covers.

4. After you turn the light out, relax by breathing deeply, in and out through your nose, making your 'out' breaths last slightly longer than your 'in' breaths. This should soon lull you slowly into a deep sleep. Zzzzz ...

HOME HELP

SKILL 52

UNSTICK CHEWING GUM

Chewing gum on your stuff can make for a sticky situation. Here's how to remove it:

1. Place the item with the chewing gum stuck to it into the freezer overnight.

2. In the morning, remove the item and take it to the sink. Use a butter knife to carefully scrape off the frozen gum.

If the item is too large to fit in a freezer, fill a plastic food bag with ice cubes and secure firmly with an elastic band. Place the bag over the gum and leave it until the gum has frozen. Carefully remove the frozen gum using a butter knife, then follow **step 3** below.

3. Use a clean cloth soaked in water and a squirt of washing-up liquid to wipe away any traces of the gum. Leave the item to dry completely, then wash as normal (see **Skill 59**).

SKILL SUGGESTION

To get chewing gum out of your hair, hold an ice cube over the affected area. When the gum hardens, pick it off with your fingers. Remove any remaining bits of gum by massaging peanut butter into the hair, then comb the area using a nit comb (or a fine-toothed comb). Wash your hair as normal (see **Skill 4**). **Warning:** Don't touch peanut butter if you have a peanut allergy.

SKILL 53

PACK SHOPPING BAGS PERFECTLY

Make carrying your shopping home disaster-free by following these five golden rules:

Rule 1. Take your own shopping bags when you go food shopping – it's better for the environment than using new ones.

Rule 2. Divide your shopping into separate bags like so:

• Toiletries and cleaners • Fruit and vegetables • Items that go in the fridge or freezer • Heavy items such as cans, bottles and sturdy packets.

Rule 3. Pack heavy items, such as potatoes, first and soft, light items, such as peaches and tomatoes, on the top.

Rule 4. If using supermarket bags to carry bottles, place one inside the other for double-strength bags.

Rule 5. When you get home, unpack the cold items first and put them in the fridge or freezer before you put the rest of the shopping away.

SKILL 54

LOOK AFTER A HOUSE PLANT

Be a green-fingered goddess and give a house plant some tender loving care. Read on to find out how:

Look at the label. This will tell you if the plant has any special requirements.

For example, cactuses like sunny windowsills; ferns like humid environments, so they like being sprinkled with water on their leaves each day; and lilies like cool conditions, so never leave one in direct sunlight.

Watering rules. Only water your plant when the soil of the plant feels almost dry. Different types of plant need different amounts of water, but most need more during the spring and summer.

Check for dead foliage. Using your fingers, gently pull off any flowers or leaves that have turned brown.

Dust it. The leaves of plants can often get dusty – this stops the plant from growing properly. To help your plant grow big and beautiful, take a damp piece of kitchen paper and smooth it along the leaves to clean them.

SKILL 55

GET THE MOST FROM YOUR PRODUCTS

Here's how to make all your tubes and bottles last longer, so you can save your precious pennies:

• Store bottles upside down when they start to run out – this will help you to get any last drops out when you want them.

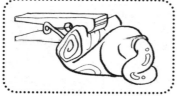

• Roll tubes up slowly from the end, pushing the dregs of the product to the opening as you go. Secure the rolled-up tube with a peg to keep it in position.

• If you think you have used the last drops out of a tube, try carefully snipping the top end off with scissors, as shown here – there is usually some left at the opening.

SKILL SUGGESTION

Buy tubs rather than bottles for things such as creams and lotions, because it's far easier to get every last bit out.

• Make bath foam or shampoo last longer by adding a very small amount of water to the last bit in the bottles.

SKILL 56

TIDY YOUR BEDROOM IN FIVE MINUTES

Can't find your bed underneath that giant clothes mountain? Tidying needn't be an all-day job – start the clock and get it done in just five minutes:

Five minutes to go. Pile any dirty clothes into the laundry basket. Hang clean clothes in your wardrobe or fold them and put them in your drawers.

Four minutes to go. Get a bin liner, and scan the room for all the items of rubbish. Put any school papers on your desk in a neat pile and pop all your stationery in a desk tidy.

Three minutes to go. Collect up all your books, DVDs and games and organize them on shelves in height order so that they look tidy. Place any jewellery and accessories in neat little boxes.

Two minutes to go.
Pick up any dirty plates, cups or bowls and take them to the kitchen to wash up later (see **Skill 68**).

One minute to go. Shake out your duvet, then smooth it down and plump up the pillows. Pop your pyjamas under the pillow and step back to admire your tidy bedroom.

SKILL 57

REMOVE A STAIN

Below are some common stains that tend to ruin clothes – unless you know these crafty stain solutions:

Stain: Glue.
What to do: If the glue is still wet, dip some cotton wool in warm water and dab the stain with it. If it is dried glue, dab it with nail polish remover, then wash the garment as normal.

Stain: Ink.
What to do: If it is on white fabric, sprinkle with salt and then rub with lemon. Rinse and wash as normal. If it is on coloured fabric, soak the stain immediately in slightly warmed milk, then rinse and wash as normal.

Stain: Tea.
What to do: Rinse the stain under the cold tap. Rub some liquid laundry detergent directly on to the stain, massaging it into the fabric. Continue massaging firmly for a minute, then rinse and wash as normal. Never use soap, as this will 'set' the stain.

Stain: Chocolate.
What to do: Place the item in the freezer for a few hours. Take it out and scrape any chocolate away with a butter knife. Scrub the area with washing-up liquid, then wash the garment as normal.

GET A JAM-JAR LID OFF

**The bread is toasting away in the toaster,
but the lid of the jam jar is stuck fast.
Try these twisty tricks to get it off:**

• Tap around the edge of the lid with the handle of a wooden spoon. This action may be enough to shift anything that is sticking it closed.

• Slide the tip of the handle of a teaspoon into any gap between the lid and the jar. You may hear a 'pop' – this releases air that is holding the lid tight.

• Run the hot tap in the kitchen and hold the jar so that water runs over the lid area. After a minute or so, turn off the tap, dry the jar with a tea towel and the lid should twist off easily.

• Put on a pair of rubber gloves and try twisting the lid off – you should get a better grip with rubber gloves on without hurting your hands.

SKILL 59

PUT ON A LOAD OF WASHING

Laundry is a real skill – get it wrong and your best white vest top will come out sludgy green and tiny. Follow this guide and take the worry out of doing the washing:

1. Separate all the dirty clothes into the following piles:

• Whites – go through this pile carefully to check that there are no stray dark socks • Colours – include pastel coloured or bright clothes • Darks – include black, navy and dark jeans.

2. Check that the pockets are empty. Hard items such as keys will damage the washing machine and tissues will leave tiny pieces of fluff all over your clothes.

3. Find the care label – this has the washing instructions on it. It is usually inside the garment, stitched into a seam. Look for a symbol – some examples of symbols are shown opposite.

 This means this item needs to be washed at 40°C.

 This means this item needs to be washed at 60°C.

 Do not wash this item in a washing machine – cool hand-wash only.

These symbols tell you the temperature of water that the garment needs, or if you can wash it at all.

 Do not wash this item – dry clean only.

4. Separate the garments within each pile into groups that should be washed at the same temperature, keeping them sorted by colour.

5. Place the first load of washing into the 'drum' of the machine and close the door.

6. Open the drawer on the front – it is usually on the top left of the machine – and fill the correct section with a scoop of washing powder or cap of liquid laundry detergent. If you use tablets, pop these directly inside the drum.

7. Pour a cap of fabric conditioner into the specified section of the drawer. Close the drawer.

8. Select the correct setting on the washing machine for the load you are washing. All washing machines will be different, but there will be a control panel on your machine that will offer you different settings. Ask an adult to help you if are still not sure.

 40°C   **DELICATES OR SYNTHETICS**   **QUICK WASH**

| **1.** Select the correct temperature. | **2.** If there is an option to select the type of fabric that the garment is made out of, do this now. | **3.** Select the type of wash, for example, 'QUICK WASH'. |

9. Press 'START'. When the washing cycle is complete, turn to **Skill 63** to find out how to hang washing out.

SKILL SUGGESTION

Washing clothes at a lower temperature than indicated on the care label won't harm them. Never wash them at a higher one though – it could shrink the items.

SKILL 60

LOAD A DISHWASHER

If you are lucky enough to have a dishwasher, learn how to use it and say bye-bye to washing-up!

PRE-PACKING

1. Throw away any excess food from plates or bowls into the waste bin.

2. Rinse each item of crockery under the tap. Check for anything that's stuck around the plughole, and remove any stray bits of food you find.

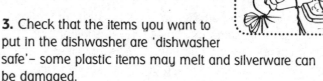

3. Check that the items you want to put in the dishwasher are 'dishwasher safe'– some plastic items may melt and silverware can be damaged.

LOAD IT RIGHT

4. Dishwashers are designed so that each item has its own special place. Use the diagram on the opposite page to help you locate where things go:

WARNING

Dishwasher designs may vary. Always check your dishwasher's instructions before loading it.

a. Place large and medium-sized plates in the narrow, slotted areas on the bottom rack.

b. Place smaller plates in the narrow, slotted racks on the top rack. Place smaller bowls along the side of the top rack.

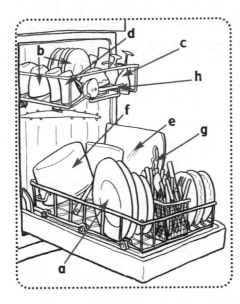

c. Place glasses face down between the spikes along the sides of the top rack.

d. Place coffee mugs upside down on the outer edges of the top rack.

e. Place plastic chopping boards along the sides on the bottom rack.

f. Pots and pans should be placed upside down on the bottom drawer.

g. Place all cutlery in the removable basket. Always put knives in the dishwasher with the blades pointing down.

h. Larger utensils should be placed flat on the top rack.

SWITCH IT ON

5. Make sure that there are no big items which will stop the 'washing arm' – found underneath the top rack – from turning.

6. Place the dishwasher tablet, powder or liquid in the space provided – usually inside a flap on the inside of the door.

7. Push the door shut and select the wash setting (quick wash, normal, and so on). Then wait for it to finish.

> **SKILL SUGGESTION**
>
> Stand well back when opening the door of a dishwasher that's just finished, or you'll get a face full of steam.

SKILL 61

DUST LIKE A CLEANING QUEEN

Dusting makes a room feel bright and clean – it also stops you sneezing! Here's how to dust a room:

1. Open any windows in the room – this will allow all the dust particles to fly out into the open, and it also gets fresh air inside.

2. Remove all objects from any shelves, such as ornaments, and carefully place them on a tray on the floor.

3. Use a feather duster to dust down the tallest places in the room – stand on a chair or the bed to reach into cobwebby corners and lampshades.

4. Dust down all other surfaces, picture frames, skirting boards and windowsills.

5. Wipe the cleared shelves with a damp cloth or some polishing spray. Gently wipe the ornaments with a soft cloth and put them back on the shelves.

6. Take items such as rugs or cushions outside and shake them out to remove the dust, then put them back in the room.

7. Use a vacuum to clean the floor area after you have finished dusting to remove any remaining dust (see **Skill 65**).

SKILL 62

SORT THE RECYCLING

**Make your household recycling routine simple
and effective – you'll be doing your family
a favour as well as the planet. Here's how:**

1. Check on your local council's website to find out which items
are accepted for recycling and which are not. Find out which day
they collect on, too.

2. Some councils provide a recycling box
(or a bag) to store recyclable items in.

If your council does not, find a large
box and place it next to the kitchen bin.

3. Write out the list of items that can be
recycled and stick it to the side of your
box. Before putting any items into the
box, you will need to prepare them first.

• Cans, bottles and plastic containers need to be rinsed out before
they can be recycled. Wear rubber gloves to do this – this will
protect your hands if items break. Be careful of any sharp edges
on cans. Leave the items to dry, then put them in the box. Bottle
lids and caps cannot be recycled.

• Flatten cardboard boxes and cereal packets, and crush drinking
cans, before popping them in the recycling box – this will save
space so that you can fit more items in to be recycled.

4. Before the collection time, take the box out of the house
and place it on the kerbside.

SKILL 63

HANG OUT LAUNDRY

If you have a washing line set up outside, make use of it to get fresh-smelling laundry. Here's how:

1. Choose a bright, blustery day for drying clothes, but keep an eye out for rain clouds at all times.

2. Take your freshly washed clothes outside. Turn each item inside out – this will stop the sun bleaching the colour out of your clothes, or whites becoming yellow.

3. Give each of your items a good shake to stop them drying with creases in. Peg T-shirts, shirts and dresses upside down. Clip a peg at either end of the seams.

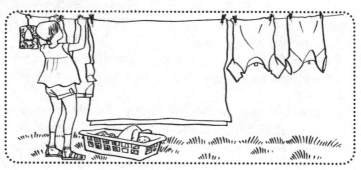

4. Peg trousers upside down with a peg in the middle of the seam of each leg.

5. Fold sheets or blankets in half and hang them over the line. Peg them at both ends.

6. When each item is completely dry, fold your washing neatly so it doesn't crease, and take it inside.

SKILL 64

CLEAR THE TABLE

What better way to thank your folks after a delicious meal than by clearing the table afterwards? Here's how to do it, waitress-style:

1. Ask if everyone has finished eating. If they have, stand up and go to each place to remove the plate rather than reaching across the table. You are less likely to drop things this way, too.

2. With your dominant hand (the one you write with), pick up the plate and place it on the other hand, cradling it in the forearm.

SKILL SUGGESTION

Don't overload yourself – it's always best to make several trips to the kitchen than to smash expensive crockery.

3. Remove the cutlery from each plate, so that it's on top of the pile of plates.

4. When you get to the kitchen, scrape all the leftovers on to one plate and throw in the waste bin.

5. When all the main plates have been removed, collect other items. Take a piece of kitchen paper or a napkin to scoop up any blobs of food.

6. Wipe down place mats and put away salt, pepper and any sauces that have been used.

SKILL 65

VACUUM YOUR BEDROOM

Once you've tidied your bedroom (see *Skill 56*), why not vacuum it for that extra-clean feeling? Follow the steps below to find out how:

1. Place bins, chairs, boxes, and all other clutter outside the room. If your duvet trails on the floor, lift it up on to the bed.

2. If your vacuum cleaner has one, attach the 'crevice nozzle' (the long, thin tool) to the end of the hose. Vacuum the edges of the room, pushing the nozzle right up against the wall.

3. Kneel down and check for stray items under the bed. Once you've removed them, vacuum underneath the bed.

4. Remove the crevice nozzle. Using the main brush head, vacuum the rest of the floor. Start from the far edges of the room and work towards the door, pushing the vacuum cleaner up and down the carpet with big, sweeping strokes.

SKILL SUGGESTION

If the vacuum isn't working well, it might be that it's full. Ask an adult to help you empty it or change the bag, then get back to work.

SKILL 66

RAKE UP LEAVES

Autumn leaves can be bad for the lawn and can look really messy. Here's the fuss-free way to clear them away:

1. Pop on a long-sleeved jumper, sturdy jeans and a pair of gardening gloves – these will protect you from any thorns or sharp stones you may come across among the leaves.

2. Using a wide, fan-shaped rake, drag the 'tines' (prongs) of the rake over the leaves on the lawn, making short strokes towards you, to make a small pile of leaves.

3. Lay an old sheet flat on the lawn beside the pile of leaves. Sweep the leaves on to the sheet using the rake.

4. Carefully, pick up all four corners of the sheet, keeping the leaves safely stowed in the middle of the sheet, and carry the bundle to the compost bin if you have one. If not, fill bin liners with them. Tie them at the top and ask an adult if your local council will collect them.

5. Repeat **steps 2** to **4** until all the leaves have been cleared from the lawn.

SKILL SUGGESTION

Choose a dry, still day to rake up leaves. You don't want a strong gust of wind ruining all your hard work!

SKILL 67

FOLD A BIG SHEET

Enlist the help of a friend, parent or sibling and follow these instructions to fold your bedding quickly and neatly, no matter what size it is:

1. Open out the sheet fully and lay it on a large, flat surface, such as a bed or a table.

2. Pick up the sheet by the bottom two corners, and ask your helper to take the top two corners.

3. Both walk backwards a few steps, holding the sheet up and your arms wide so that it is stretched out.

The following steps need to be done by you and your helper at the same time, so at each step, give them the instruction and a nod to say, 'Go!'

4. Bring your hands together so that the corners you are holding touch.

5. Keep holding the corners together with one hand, then take away your dominant hand (the one you write with) so that the sheet is hanging down from the corner.

6. Reach down and grab the bottom of the piece you are holding. Pull it out so the sheet is flat.

Now bring this hand up level with the other.

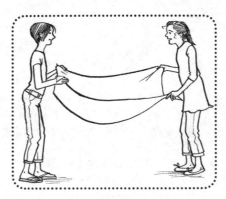

7. Holding your corners, walk towards each other and meet at the middle so that your ends and the helper's ends touch. One person takes the top two corners and the other takes the bottom two corners.

8. Walk back again to stretch out the folded sheet and repeat **steps 5** to **7** until the sheet is folded neatly enough to be put away.

SKILL 68

DO THE WASHING-UP

Follow these steps to get the dishes sparkling clean:

1. Put on rubber gloves – they protect your hands from the drying effects of hot, soapy water.

2. Half fill the sink or bowl with hot water (make sure it's not too hot or you'll burn your hands). Add one squirt of washing-up liquid.

3. Wash glasses and cups first as they need the hottest, cleanest water. Use a brush to clean inside and out, paying special attention to the rims. Rinse each glass under the hot tap and place upside down on a draining rack.

4. Put all the cutlery in the sink, then use a sponge or cloth to clean each individual piece. Rinse under the hot tap then leave it to dry with blades and prongs pointing downwards in the cutlery holder on the rack. Be extra careful when handling sharp knives.

5. Clean the plates and bowls using the sponge or cloth. If the water is getting murky, pour it away and run a fresh bowl, adding another squirt of washing-up liquid.

6. Using a scouring pad, scrub off any caked-on food from pots and pans. Rinse and place upside down on the draining rack.

SKILL SUGGESTION

Leave the washing-up to dry naturally (no tea towels required) if you have the space – this is a more hygienic way to do it. Polish glasses and cutlery with a clean cloth once they are dry.

PACK A SUITCASE

Here's how to get everything you need for a holiday neatly packed into a case:

1. Write a list of everything you want to pack – you can tick each item off when it is safely packed in your suitcase. For example, for each day, you will need underwear, a pair of shorts, a skirt or trousers, a vest top or T-shirt, and another top for the evening, plus a jumper. Pack a swimsuit if there's a pool or beach, and enough pairs of shoes for the trip.

2. Open up your case and place it on your bed. Lay out each item that you want to pack on the bed.

3. Fold up bulkier, non-crease items first, such as towels, denim items, jumpers and cardigans and place them in the suitcase. Rolling items up takes up less room if you are tight on space. Fold delicate items such as vest tops and place them on top of the heavier items.

4. Wedge shoes and sandals in around the sides with their soles flat against the lining of the case.

5. Pack toiletries inside a plastic bag, in case they leak.

SKILL SUGGESTION

If you're flying, pack a change of underwear, a toothbrush and a top in your hand luggage, just in case your suitcase goes missing.

SKILL 70

CLEAN A WINDOW

Cleaning windows is a great skill to learn and one of those chores that will really impress your parents. Here's how to get that glass perfect:

SAFETY FIRST

Stick to downstairs windows. Leave the high-up windows and hard-to-reach spots to the professionals.

1. Pick a cloudy day to wash the windows – sunshine will dry them too quickly, leaving streaks on the glass.

2. Put on rubber gloves and half fill a bucket with warm water. Add several good splashes of distilled (clear) vinegar and mix well.

3. Start by doing the outside of the windows. Soak a cloth in the water and rub the window across and then down.

4. Use a squeegee – a tool with a rubber blade in – to wipe away any excess water. Wipe down the window, in a zigzag movement from side to side.

5. Use a dry chamois leather (or a soft, clean cloth) to dry the glass and make it shine. Rub it all over the window in circular movements.

6. Lay down sheets of newspaper underneath the windows inside the house to catch drips.

7. Repeat **steps 3** to **5** on the inside.

SKILL 71

FOLD A T-SHIRT

Keep your T-shirt drawer in order with this neat folding technique:

1. Lay your T-shirt out, face down on flat surface. Run your hand over it to smooth out any wrinkles.

2. Fold one side over from the shoulder seam in towards the middle of the shirt.

3. Repeat with the other side. Fold both the sleeves back over themselves so that their corners reach the edges of the shirt.

shoulder seam

4. Pull the bottom half of the T-shirt up until the bottom seam touches just below the collar.

5. Carefully turn the folded T-shirt over and place neatly in your T-shirt drawer.

SKILL SUGGESTION

While T-shirts can be folded and put away, always hang dresses, shirts or blouses in your wardrobe to stop them getting creased. Use one hanger per item and do up the top few buttons of a shirt or blouse to stop them falling off the hanger. Fold trousers in half (one leg on top of the other) and hang them over a coat hanger in your wardrobe.

SKILL 72

PUT ON A DUVET COVER

Putting a duvet cover on doesn't mean you have to get tangled up in linen. Follow the method below to find out how to beat the bedding into shape:

1. Remove the dirty duvet cover and pop it in the laundry basket.

2. Lay the duvet out flat on the floor and turn the clean duvet cover inside out.

3. Put your hands inside the duvet cover, until you can reach the two corners furthest from the open end.

4. Grip hold of these corners tightly, one in each hand. Your hands should now be gloved by the duvet.

5. Pick up the two corners of the duvet with your gloved hands, as shown.

6. Hold both duvet corners and duvet cover corners in the air and shake hard until the cover reaches the bottom ends of the duvet.

7. Close the fastenings at the bottom end of the duvet.

SKILL 73

MOP THE FLOOR

Here's how to make your kitchen sparkle underfoot:

1. Move any portable items, such as bins or chairs, out of the room, then vacuum the area you want to mop (see **Skill 65**).

2. Half fill a bucket with warm water. Pop on some rubber gloves, then add the correct amount of floor cleaner according to the instructions on the bottle.

3. Dip a mop into the bucket and squeeze out the excess water. If you have a sponge mop, pull the lever on it down to squeeze out excess water. If it is a rag mop, use your hands to wring it out into the bucket.

4. Start mopping in the furthest points of the room from the door and work backwards – this is so that you do not need to walk in the parts that you have just cleaned.

SKILL SUGGESTION

If your mop is a rag type, use a figure-of-eight motion to wipe the floor. If it is a sponge mop, drag it in a straight line.

5. Dip your mop back in the water to clean it, wringing it out well each time. Pour the water away if it becomes murky and half fill a fresh bucket of hot water and cleaning solution.

6. Ban family members and pets from entering the room until the floor is completely dry.

EMERGENCY
SKILLS

SKILL 74

CALL THE EMERGENCY SERVICES

There may be a time when you need to contact the police, ambulance, or fire services. Here's how to get help quickly and efficiently:

1. Safety first. If there is a fire, get outside. If you have to get out on to a road, make sure you are in a safe place away from traffic.

2. Dial 999. It is free to call 999 from mobile phones, land lines and telephone boxes. An operator will ask you what number you are calling from. If you get cut off they will ring you back.

3. Police, fire or ambulance? The operator will ask you if you need the police, fire services or an ambulance.

4. Where are you? The operator will ask you the address and postcode of where you are. If you don't know the full address, look for a street name or a recognizable landmark, such as a group of shops or a pub. If you are in a house with other people, ask someone to wait outside to flag the emergency services down. Leave the front door open – this will save time when the emergency services arrive.

5. Explain clearly. You will be asked a series of questions. If someone is hurt you may be asked questions such as, 'Is the person still breathing?' They will then instruct you on what to do until help arrives. You may be asked to stay on the line until they reach you.

> **WARNING**
>
> Never dial 999 unless it is an emergency – you could put others' lives at risk.

SKILL 75

GET TO GRIPS WITH FIRE SAFETY

If a fire breaks out in your home, follow these rules:

1. Stay calm. Reacting calmly and sensibly will help you get to safety as quickly as possible.

2. Get outside. Leave the building and walk to a safe place away from the fire. Do not take anything with you – it could slow you down. Do not run – you could trip over and get stuck inside. Never use a lift – it may break because of the fire.

3. Warm door warning. When moving to get outside, feel any doors before you open them. If the door is warm, there could be a fire on the other side, so do not open it. Take an alternative route to safety.

4. Keep low. If there is a lot of smoke, crawl on all fours as you move – the air is clearer lower down. If you can, cover your mouth and nose with a damp cloth. This will make the air cleaner to breath.

5. Call 999. As soon as you are clear of the building call the emergency services (see **Skill 74**).

> ### WARNING
> Never go back into a building until the fire service has told you it is safe to do so.

SKILL 76

ROAD SAFETY DRILL

Find a safe place to cross, such as a pelican or zebra crossing, then follow the rules below:

Stop just before you reach the kerb.

Look in both directions for any approaching vehicles. Watch out for motorbikes and bicycles, as well as cars.

Listen carefully for any engine noise. Never be tempted to nip across the road if you hear a vehicle in the distance – it is difficult to judge how fast it is going.

Arrive alive. When it is safe to cross, walk across the road in a straight line. Don't dawdle or play around in the middle of the road – it could cost you your life.

Never cross on the brow of a hill, between parked cars, or on a corner that you can't see around. Look for a zebra or pelican crossing instead.

SKILL SUGGESTION

Make sure you can be seen at night by wearing bright, reflective clothing or a bright hat. You could even add reflective stickers and clips to your bag.

TIE A SLING

**Show off your nursing skills by tying a sling
to support an injured arm. Here's how:**

1. To make a sling, find a large square-shaped piece of fabric and a safety pin. Fold the fabric in half diagonally to make a triangle.

2. Ask the patient to bend their injured arm and hold it across their chest.

3. Place the triangle across the front of their body, under the injured arm. The longest side of the triangle should be next to the patient's fingers, with one end placed over the shoulder.

4. Bring the bottom point over the injured arm and up to the opposite shoulder. Gently tie the ends together behind the patient's neck in a double knot.

5. Check that the sling isn't too tight and that the patient's wrist is supported. You should be able to see the fingers poking out from the fabric, as shown here.

6. Tuck any loose fabric around the elbow and carefully secure it in place with the safety pin.

SKILL 78

TAKE A PULSE

Taking a pulse is a useful first-aid skill to learn, because it tells you how fast an injured person's heart is beating. Read on to find your own pulse:

1. Hold one hand out, palm up, with the arm relaxed.

2. Put the index and middle finger of your other hand together and gently press on to the wrist at the base of your thumb.

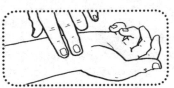

You should be able to feel your pulse in 'beats'– this is actually the blood moving underneath the skin.

SKILL SUGGESTION

If you can't find your pulse in your wrist, try to find it in your neck using your fingers.

3. Once you have found your pulse, you can check the rate at which your heart is beating. To do this, you will need to look at a clock or watch with a second hand. When the second hand reaches 12, start counting how many times your pulse beats. Stop when the second hand reaches six, then double it to find out how many beats your pulse makes in a minute.

What's normal? A 'resting heart rate' – a person's heart rate when they have just woken up in the morning – can range between 60 to 100 beats per minute for children. If you are worried about your pulse rate, tell an adult.

SKILL 79

COPE IF YOU ARE LOST

If you get separated from your friends when you're out and about, follow these rules:

SKILL SUGGESTION

Write down your mum or dad's mobile phone number and a few of your friends' numbers, too. Keep their numbers with you at all times and some coins for a payphone.

1. Don't panic. Breathe deeply for a few moments – this will calm you down and help you to think clearly.

2. If you have a prearranged meeting place where your friends might look for you, head straight there.

If not, continue to **step 3**.

3. Find somewhere safe to wait, such as a busy café. Phone your friends and family to tell them where you are. Don't wander off to look for your friends – it is much safer to stay in a busy, public place.

4. If there is nowhere safe to wait, or you can't find a pay phone to use, tell a responsible adult, such as a police officer or a shop manager, what has happened and ask them to contact your family.

WARNING

Never get in a car with strangers or go off with them — even if they say they'll take you home.

SKILL 80

TREAT A BEE STING

Ah, summer fun playing outside ... until a bee spoils your fun with a painful sting! Here's how to treat it:

1. First you need to remove the sting that the bee has left behind inside your skin.

Bee stings have tiny hooks called barbs on them which can get stuck in your skin if you just pull them out.

To avoid this, scrape the edge of a ruler or a bank card in a scooping motion across the sting to gradually ease it out.

2. Wash the area with soap and water, and dry it gently.

3. Wrap some ice cubes or an ice pack in a tea towel and wrap it around the stung area.

4. Rest the area that has been stung and elevate it if you can – this will reduce any swelling.

WARNING

If your eyes, lips or tongue swell, or you feel dizzy or it's hard to breathe, you may be allergic to the sting. Get help from an adult immediately.

SKILL 81

TREAT A CUT OR GRAZE

Leading a fun life means that you might get cuts and grazes from time to time. Here's how to clean them quickly and hygienically:

WARNING

If the cut is more that 1 cm long, or deep, seek medical attention immediately.

CLEAN UP

1. Wash your hands in soapy water and dry thoroughly.

2. Rinse the wounded area under lukewarm, running tap water.

3. If there are any pieces of gravel or dirt in the cut or graze, ask an adult for help.

4. Use a clean towel to gently pat the area dry. If the area is still bleeding, apply gentle pressure to the wound using a clean cloth – this will slow the blood flow to the wound.

5. If the cut or graze continues to bleed, raise the wounded area – this should stop the bleeding.

6. Once the bleeding has stopped, apply a small blob of antiseptic cream to the area using a clean finger.

COVER UP

7. Choose a plaster with an absorbant pad that's large enough to cover the whole of the area of the cut.

8. Put it over the cut and gently press the sticky areas down to fix it in place.

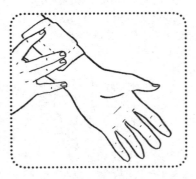

SKILL SUGGESTION

If you don't have a plaster large enough to cover the wound, you can cover the area using a non-fluffy bandage instead. Use a safety pin to fix the bandage in place.

WARNING

If blood seeps through the plaster or bandage, apply another one over the top. If the bleeding continues, remove both dressings, apply fresh ones and seek medical attention immediately.

SKILL 82

TREAT A BURN

If you burn or scald your skin, you need to act fast to stop more damage occurring. Here's how:

1. Get well away from the cause of the burn.

2. Run the cold tap, until the water is cool, but make sure it isn't too cold. Be careful not to have the tap turned on fully – the pressure of the water might damage the skin further.

WARNING

If the burn is bigger than a postage stamp, or near the mouth area, or if the skin is broken, do not attempt to treat it yourself – seek medical attention immediately.

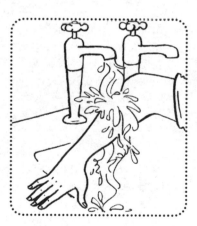

3. Place the burned area under the cool water. If the burned area is on your leg, use the bath tap or shower instead.

4. Hold the burned area under the running water for at least 15 minutes – you can time this using a clock or watch.

5. Loosely rest a non-fluffy bandage or a dampened dressing over the burn and fix in place using a safety pin.

SKILL 83

STOP MUSCLE CRAMP

Cramp can take you by surprise and can be very painful when it strikes. Read on to find out all about cramp and how to stop it in its tracks:

WHAT IS CRAMP?

★ Cramp is a muscle spasm. It can last just a few seconds or for several minutes. It often occurs when muscles get tired, so is most common during or after exercise. It does sometimes strike at other times too, such as when you are sleeping ... ouch!

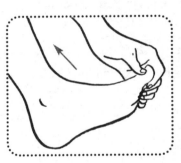

LEG CRAMP

If the cramp is in your lower leg, take your shoes off and flex your foot up towards your shin, as shown here. This will stretch the muscles in your leg and stop them from cramping.

ARM CRAMP

Lift the affected arm above your head and bend it, reaching behind you. Use the other hand to gently push the arm further down behind you by pressing on your forearm just below the elbow.

POST-CRAMP CARE

• Work out what is causing the cramp – for example, a pain in your hand from writing for a long time, or an arm-ache from playing tennis. Once you have worked out the cause, take a break!

• Massage the area where the cramp occurred by applying pressure with the hand and moving the hand in small circles.

PREVENT CRAMP

Stretching your muscles before exercise stops cramp before it strikes. Here's how to stretch your legs:

1. Place the palms of your hands flat against a wall. Stand up and take a big step back with the right foot, then bend the left leg. Keep the right foot flat on the floor and straighten the leg until you can feel the stretch in your leg. Hold this position while counting up to ten.

2. Next, bring your right foot up until the heel of your shoe touches the back of your leg. Hold your ankle in this position and count to ten. Repeat **steps 1** and **2** with the other leg.

SKILL SUGGESTION

Cramp often occurs due to dehydration, so drink plenty of water or squash before and after doing exercise. Eating one banana a day can also help keep cramp at bay.

SKILL 84

STOP A NOSEBLEED

If a nosebleed strikes, follow the steps below to stop it as soon as it starts:

1. Position an empty bucket on the floor just in front of a chair.

2. Sit down on the chair and lean forward slightly so that your nose is directly above the bucket, so that it will catch the dripping blood.

3. Firmly pinch the softest part of your nose – just above the nostrils and below the bony ridge – with your thumb and index finger. Breathe through your mouth.

4. Stay in this position for 10 to 15 minutes. The bleeding should stop during this period.

5. Avoid blowing your nose or bending down for a few hours after the bleeding stops.

SKILL SUGGESTION

To avoid nosebleeds, only blow your nose when you need to and never blow too hard.

WARNING

If the bleeding doesn't stop after 30 minutes, or you start to feel light-headed, seek medical attention immediately.

SKILL 85

HELP SOMEONE WHO IS CHOKING

Learn what to do if your friend is choking and you could be a real life-saver one day:

1. If she can still speak and breathe, tell her to keep trying to clear her throat herself by coughing. The object should pop out of her mouth or throat. If this doesn't work, continue to **step 2**.

2. Explain that you are going to try to remove the blockage using five sharp whacks to her back.

> ### WARNING
>
> If the person choking cannot speak or breathe, call 999 (see **Skill 74**) and fetch an adult immediately – do not attempt to deal with it yourself.

3. Stand behind her and lean her forward slightly. Give her five short whacks on the back between the shoulder blades, using the heel of your hand.

Stop after each whack to see if the blockage has cleared.

4. If the blockage has still not cleared, dial 999 immediately (see **Skill 74**).

SKILL 86

BE RECOVERY READY

If you come across someone who is unconscious, call 999 immediately (see *Skill 74*) and tell the operator that you need an ambulance. The operator may ask you to put the person into the 'recovery position' – the safest position for the body to be in until help arrives.

Be ready for a real emergency and practise putting a friend into the recovery position:

1. Kneel down next to the friend who is pretending to be the injured casualty.

2. Move her arm that is nearest to you into an 'L' shape with the back of her hand on the ground.

3. Put your palm in her other hand and move it up so that the back of her hand is against her face. Keep your hand there.

4. With your other hand, pull her knee that is furthest away from you up, so that it is bent, with the foot on the floor.

5. Holding her bent knee, roll her body towards you, so that she is now lying on their side, as shown here.

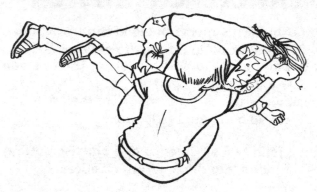

6. Gently remove your hand from underneath her face and tilt her head back slightly.

7. Lift her chin up so that she can breathe easily. In a real-life emergency, stay with her until the ambulance arrives.

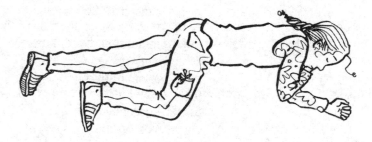

WARNING

Never put an injured person into the recovery position unless you have been told to do so by a medical professional or a 999 operator. If a person has hurt their spine, for example by falling, putting them in the recovery position might cause more damage.

REMOVE A SPLINTER

Splinters are little pieces of wood that really get under your skin. Here's how to get one out:

1. Wash your hands, then wash the area around the splinter.

2. Stand under a light or by a window, and use a magnifying glass or a mirror to identify exactly where the splinter is. Once you have located it, use a clean pair of tweezers to gently pull the splinter out.

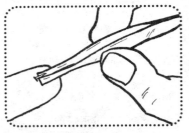

To do this, press the tweezers just under where the splinter is poking out. Hold the end of the splinter firmly in the tips of the tweezers and pull in the opposite direction that it went in.

Don't press down directly on the splinter – this could push it deeper into your skin.

3. Once you have removed the splinter, wash and clean the whole area with mild antiseptic.

SKILL SUGGESTION

If the splinter isn't budging, have a hot bath or shower – the steam will open the skin's pores – then try again. If it still won't come out, ask an adult for help.

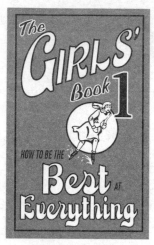
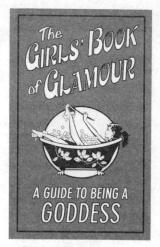

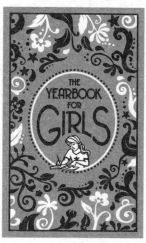